Rajiv Jansen ASSOUENE LENGO

Computers for beginners

Rajiv Jansen ASSOUENE LENGO

Computers for beginners

A complete guide to the basics of computing and essential concepts

ScienciaScripts

Cover image: www.ingimage.com

This book is a translation from the original published under ISBN 978-620-3-45949-4.

Publisher:
Sciencia Scripts
is a trademark of
Dodo Books Indian Ocean Ltd. and OmniScriptum S.R.L publishing group

120 High Road, East Finchley, London, N2 9ED, United Kingdom
Str. Armeneasca 28/1, office 1, Chisinau MD-2012, Republic of Moldova, Europe
Printed at: see last page
ISBN: 978-620-6-29132-9

CONTENTS

PREFACE

This book offers a comprehensive and accessible introduction to computing for beginners, covering essential concepts, commonly used tools and current trends. It will enable readers to get to grips with the basics and feel more comfortable using computers, the Internet and software. It is designed to be a practical and educational guide, with concrete examples and practical advice to facilitate learning. Whether you're a student, a professional or simply someone who wants to understand computers better, you've come to the right place.

CHAPTER 1: INTRODUCTION TO COMPUTERS

1. What is IT?

Computer science is a field of study and application that concerns the design, development, use and management of information systems, including computers, software, networks and data. Computer science encompasses many aspects, such as programming, database management, computer security, web design, artificial intelligence, social networks, video games, virtual reality and many others.

2. History of computing

The history of computing goes back several centuries, but it has undergone a rapid and significant evolution over the last few decades. The first mechanical devices, such as the abacus and slide rule, were used to perform mathematical calculations.

John von Neumann in front of his machine

In the 19th century, Charles Babbage designed the Analytical Machine, considered the first programmable computer. In the 20th century, with the advent of vacuum tubes and transistors, electronic computers were developed and began to be used for military, scientific and commercial applications.

Charles Babbage's analytical machine

The first scientific article in the history of computing

3. The importance of IT in everyday life

The importance of computers in everyday life has become inescapable in modern society. Computers are used in almost every aspect of daily life, for communication, education, work, leisure, health, transport, finance, online shopping and much more. Computer software and applications enable information management, problem solving, content creation and connectivity with the rest of the world. IT has transformed the way we live, work and interact with our environment, and continues to evolve rapidly, opening up new opportunities and challenges for modern society.

CHAPTER 2: COMPUTER OPERATION

Computers are electronic devices designed to process and manipulate information automatically and rapidly. Their operation relies on several key components, such as the processor, memory, storage, input/output peripherals and software.

Here are the main stages in the operation of a computer:

- Data input : Computers receive data in the form of inputs from peripheral devices such as keyboards, mice, scanners, microphones and so on. Data can also be transferred from other devices or networks.
- Processing: Once the input data has been received, the computer's processor executes instructions to process the data. The processor is the computer's brain, responsible for executing calculation, logic and control operations.
- Memory: Data and the instructions needed to process it are temporarily stored in the computer's memory, also known as RAM (Random Access Memory).

The memory allows rapid access to the data required for processing.

- Storage: Data can also be stored permanently on storage devices such as hard disks, SSDs (Solid State Drives), USB sticks and so on. These devices enable data to be retained even when the computer is switched off.
- Data output : Once the data has been processed, the results are displayed or transferred to output devices such as screen, printer, speakers, etc., for viewing or use by the user.

- Software : Software, also known as programs, are instructions written in computer code that are executed by the processor to perform specific tasks. Software can be operating systems, applications, games, web browsers and so on.
- Communication: Computers can also communicate with each other via networks, such as the Internet, to exchange data and share resources.
- All these steps are repeated in a loop to enable continuous operation of a computer and the execution of tasks requested by the user.

1. Computer components :

Computers are made up of several hardware elements, called components, which work together to enable them to function. Here is a list of the main components of a typical computer:

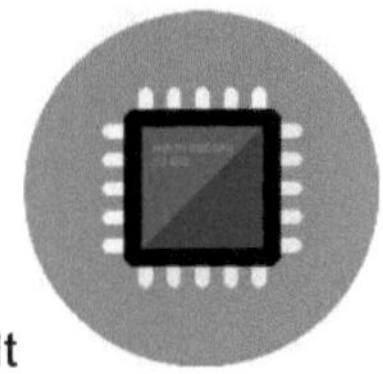

a- Processor (CPU): This is the computer's brain, responsible for executing instructions and calculation operations. It interprets software instructions and performs the necessary processing tasks.

ITEL Core i7 processor

b- Random Access Memory (RAM): This is temporary memory used to store data and instructions being used by the processor. It allows rapid access to the data required for processing.

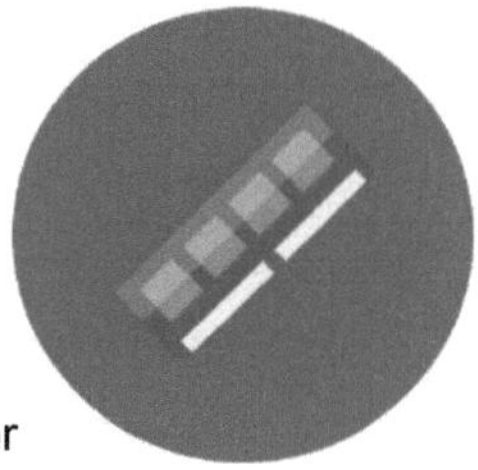

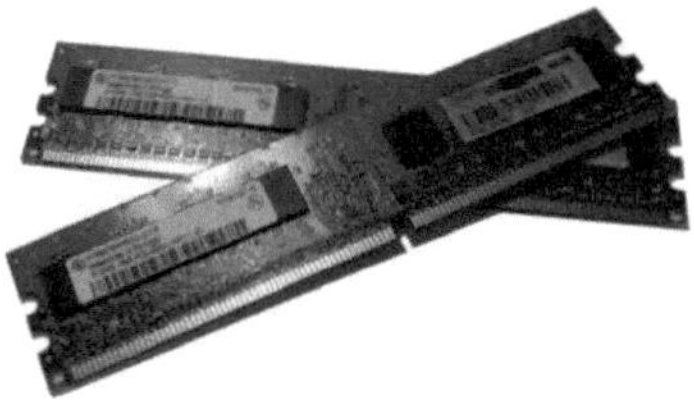

RAM strip

c- Hard Disk Drive (HDD) or Solid State Drive (SSD): These are storage devices used to retain data permanently, even when the computer is switched off. HDDs use magnetic platters to store data, while SSDs use flash memory.

Hard disk

SATA external hard drives SSD external hard disk

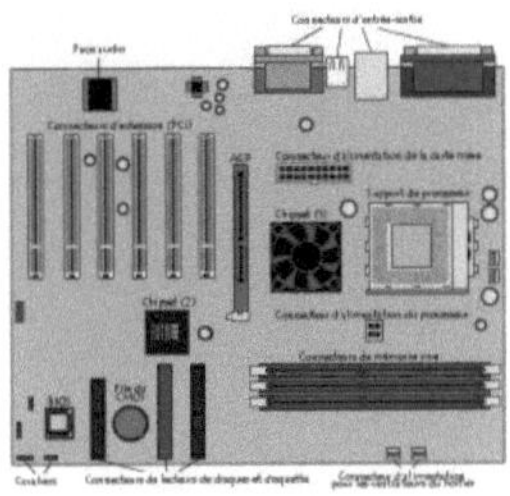

d- Motherboard: This is the computer's main printed circuit board, linking all the components together. It contains connectors and circuits to enable communication between

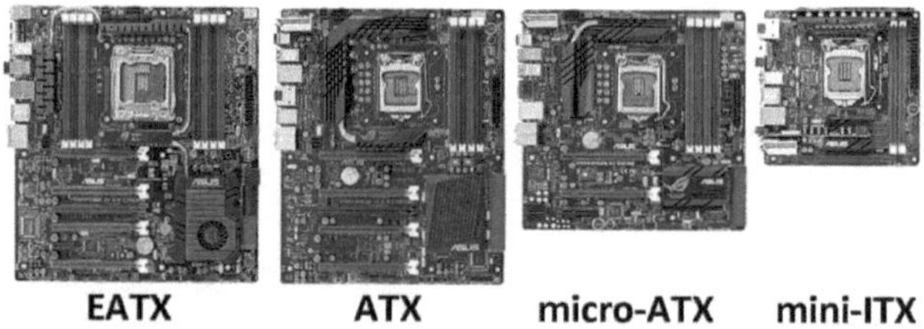

the processor, memory, storage devices, expansion cards and other components.

Motherboard size

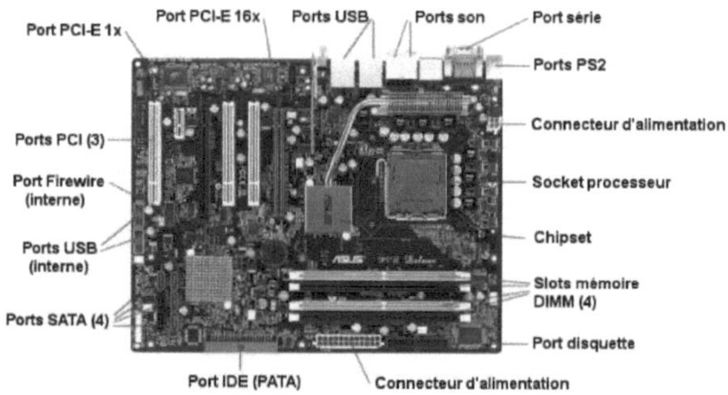

e- Graphics card: This is an expansion card responsible for managing the graphics display. It displays images, videos and games on the computer screen.

f- A component that supplies the electrical energy needed to power the computer's components.

g- Input/output peripherals: These are devices such as the keyboard, mouse, monitor, printer, speakers, microphones, etc., which enable the user to interact with the computer and receive information as output.

h- These are additional cards that can be added to the motherboard to add specific functionality to the computer, such as a network card, sound card, Wi-Fi card, etc.

i- Casing: This is the case or chassis that houses all the computer's hardware components and protects them from damage.

HP enclosure

j- Software: These are computer programs, such as operating systems, applications, games, web browsers, etc., that are installed on the computer to enable specific tasks to be carried out.

These are the main components of a computer, but there are many other components and accessories that can be added according to the user's needs and requirements.

2. Understanding the Operating System :

The operating system (OS) is the essential software that manages a computer's hardware and software resources. It is responsible for coordinating and managing computer activities, enabling users to interact with the computer and run applications.

Here are the main aspects of how an operating system works:

- The operating system manages the computer's hardware resources, such as the processor, memory, hard disk, input/output devices and so on. It allocates resources to the various applications running and ensures their efficient use.

- The operating system provides a user interface enabling users to interact with the computer, usually through a desktop, taskbar, menus, windows, etc. It also enables applications to be run, files and folders to be managed, and system settings to be configured. It also allows users to run applications, manage files and folders, and configure system settings.

- File management: The operating system manages files and folders on the hard disk or other storage devices. It lets you create, modify, copy, move and delete files, as well as organize files in a hierarchical folder structure.

Folder Personal folder File

- Process management: The operating system manages processes, which are the programs running on the computer. It allocates the necessary resources to each process, monitors their execution, enables their communication and ensures their proper termination.

- User and security management: The operating system allows you to create and manage user accounts, with different levels of authorization to access the computer's resources and functions. It also ensures security by protecting data, managing access rights and detecting and preventing potential threats.

User

- Network management: In modern operating systems, network management is also a built-in feature. It enables you to manage network connections, configure network parameters, access network resources and establish communications via the Internet or other networks.

- Driver management : The operating system manages drivers, which are software programs that enable communication between the hardware and the operating system. It recognizes, installs and updates the drivers required to operate the computer's hardware components.

In short, the operating system is responsible for the overall management of the computer, enabling users to interact with the computer, managing hardware and software resources, ensuring security and user management, and facilitating the execution of applications and processes.

3. Using input and output devices :

Input and output devices are hardware components that enable users to interact with a computer by providing data as input and receiving information as output. Here are some examples of commonly used input and output devices:

a- **Input devices**: these are hardware devices that enable the user to supply data or commands to a computer.

Here are some common examples of input devices:

- **Keyboard**: Allows you to enter text, numbers, symbols and commands using the keyboard keys.

Wired keypad

- Mouse: Moves the cursor around the screen and clicks on objects to interact with applications and windows.

Wireless mouse

- Scanner: scans documents or images and transfers them as digital data to the computer.

- Microphone: Allows sounds to be recorded and converted into audio data for use in applications such as voice recognition or sound recording.

b- **Output devices**: these are hardware devices that enable the computer to transmit data or information in the form of outputs to the user or other external devices.

Here are some common examples of output devices:

- Screen: Displays visual information generated by the computer, including images, text, videos, etc.

Screen (Monitor)

- Printer: Allows you to print documents, images or other content on paper or other physical media.

EPSON JET D'ENCRE printer

LASER CANON printer

- Speakers: Used to broadcast sound generated by the computer, including music, system sounds, videos, etc.

Speaker

- Headset: For private audio listening, including voice calls, music and games.

c- Input-output peripherals

Also known as I/O peripherals, are hardware devices that can both receive data as input and send data as output to a computer. They therefore enable the user to interact with the computer by providing input and receiving output. Here are some common examples of I/O devices:

- Touchscreen: combines the functionality of an input device and an output device, as it allows the user to provide input by directly touching the screen, and receive output in the form of images or text displayed on the screen.

- External hard disk: can be used to transfer data to a computer (input) or to back up data from a computer (output).

- Memory card reader: reads and writes data to memory cards, commonly used in cameras, smartphones and other devices, to transfer data to or from a computer.

- Modem: used to receive data input from the Internet and send data output to the Internet to establish a network connection.

- Graphical pen display: Allows the user to provide input by writing or drawing directly on the screen with a stylus, and receive output in the form of images or text displayed on the screen.

- Webcam: Can be used to capture input video or images and send them to the computer, and to display output video or images to the user.

These are just a few examples of input/output peripherals, and there are many more to choose from, depending on the specific needs and requirements of the computer and the task in hand. They enable bidirectional communication between the user and the computer, facilitating interaction and data management between the two.

The use of these input and output devices depends on the user's interaction with the computer and the specific needs of the application or task in hand. They enable communication with the computer by providing input and receiving output, facilitating user-computer interaction and enabling a variety of computer tasks to be carried out.

CHAPTER 3: OPERATING SYSTEMS

1. The main operating systems

There are several operating systems (OS) widely used in the computing world. Here are some of the main operating systems:

- Microsoft Windows: This is an operating system developed by Microsoft and widely used in personal computers (PCs) and servers. The most common versions of Windows are Windows 10 (for PCs) and Windows Server (for servers).

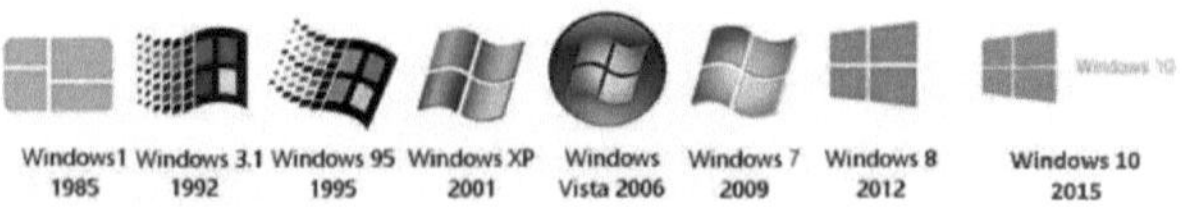

- macOS: This is the operating system developed by Apple for its Mac computers. macOS is known for its elegant, user-friendly interface, as well as its tight integration with Apple products such as iPhone, iPad and iCloud.

- Linux: This is an open-source operating system based on the Linux kernel. There are many popular Linux distributions, including Ubuntu, Fedora, Debian and CentOS, which are widely used on servers, workstations and embedded systems.

- Android: This is an open-source operating system based on the Linux kernel, developed by Google and widely used in smartphones, tablets and other mobile devices. Android is also used in many other connected devices such as smart TVs, smartwatches and Internet of Things (IoT) devices.

- iOS: This is the operating system developed by Apple exclusively for its mobile devices, such as the iPhone, iPad and iPod Touch. iOS is renowned for its user-friendliness and high level of security.

- UNIX: This is a multi-tasking, multi-user operating system originally developed by AT&T Bell Labs in the 1960s. UNIX has been widely used in server systems and workstations, and has been the basis for many other operating systems, including Linux and macOS.

There are also other, less commonly used operating systems, such as FreeBSD, OpenBSD, Solaris and others. The choice of operating system depends on the specific needs of the user or company, hardware compatibility, required applications and other factors.

2. Operating system navigation

Navigating an operating system depends on the specific operating system you're using, as each operating system has its own set of user interfaces and features. However, here are a few general concepts to help you understand how to navigate an operating system:

- Desktop: The desktop is the main interface of an operating system, where you can access various applications, folders and files. It can contain icons, shortcuts, toolbars and other visual elements to help you interact with your operating system.

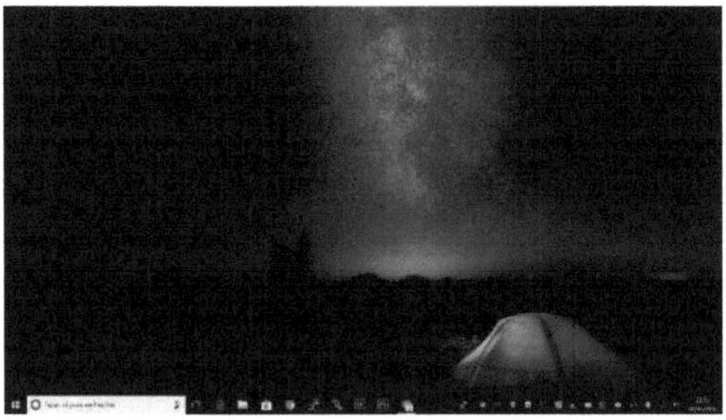

- Start menu or Dock: Some operating systems, such as Windows and macOS, have a Start menu or Dock, respectively, which lets you access applications, folders, files and other operating system features. You can click on items in the Start menu or Dock to open applications or access other functions.

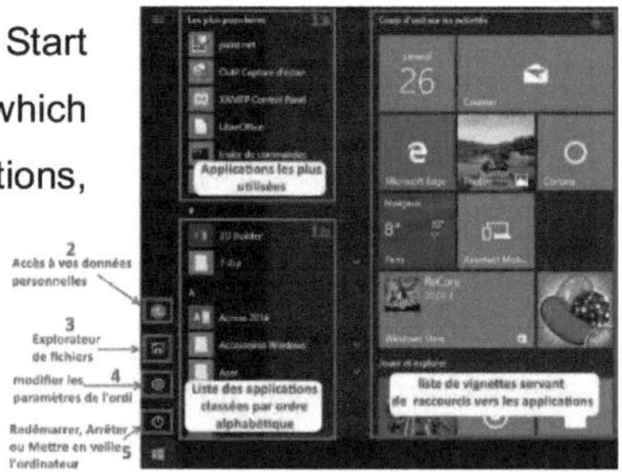

- File Explorer or Finder : File Explorer in Windows or Finder in macOS are tools that let you navigate through the files and folders on your operating system. You can use these tools to create, move, copy, delete and rename files and folders, as well as organize your digital content.

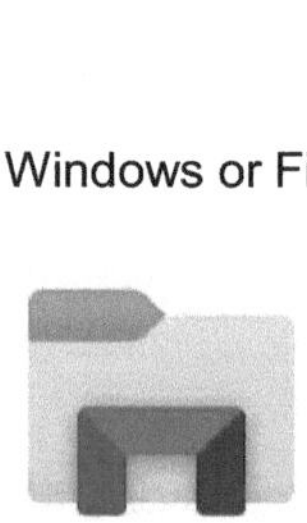

- Windows and tabs : Modern operating systems allow you to open multiple windows or tabs to display different applications or folders at the same time. You can use the minimize, maximize and close buttons to manage open applications and files in use.

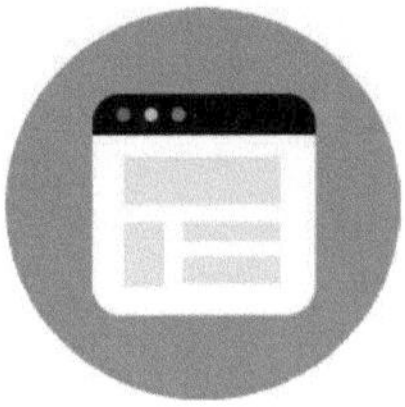

Window Tab

- Menu bars, toolbars and keyboard shortcuts: Operating systems often offer menu bars, toolbars and keyboard shortcuts for quick access to certain operating system or application functions or commands. You can use these items to perform common actions, such as searching for files, copying and pasting content, and changing system settings.

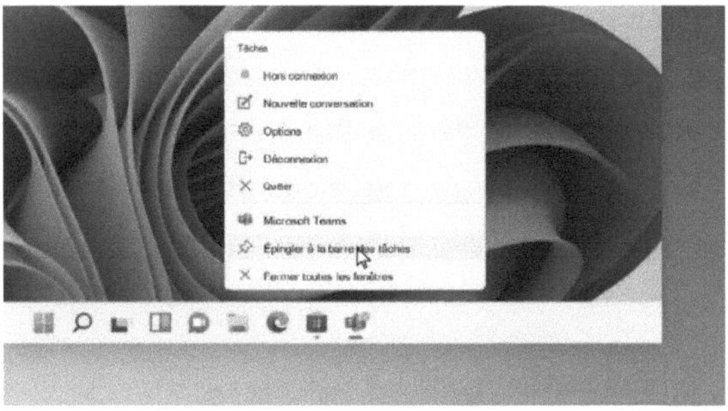

Toolbars

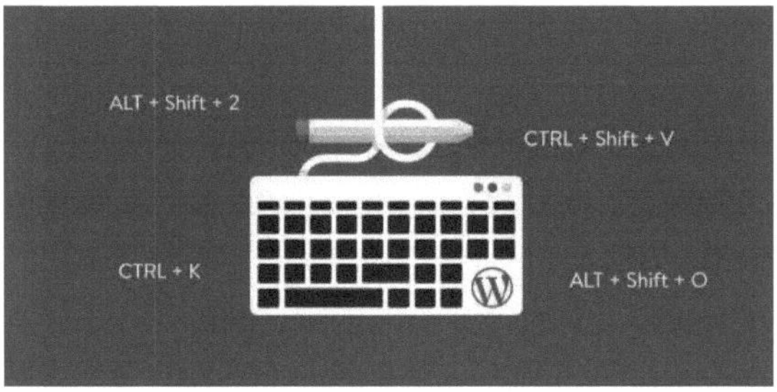

Keyboard shortcuts

- System settings: Operating systems generally have system settings that allow you to customize various configuration options, such as display preferences, network settings, user accounts, software updates and much more.  You can access these system settings from the operating system's user interface to adjust the settings to suit your needs.

It's important to note that navigation within an operating system may vary according to operating system version, computer configuration, user settings and installed applications. We therefore recommend that you consult the specific documentation for the operating system you are using to find out more about the navigation features specific to that system.

3. File and folder management

File and folder management is an essential part of using an operating system. It allows you to organize, create, modify, move, copy and delete files and folders on your computer. Here are some basic concepts to help you understand file and folder management:

- Files: Files are data units containing digital information, such as text documents, images, videos, audio files, spreadsheets, presentations and so on. Files are generally identified by a file name and extension (for example, "my_document.txt" where "my_document" is the file name and ".txt" is the file extension).
- Folders: Folders are containers that allow you to organize and group your files in a logical way. Folders can contain other folders and files, allowing you to create a hierarchical structure to organize your files according to your own filing system.

- File Explorer or Finder : File Explorer in Windows or Finder in macOS are tools that let you navigate through the files and folders on your operating system, create new folders, copy, move and delete files and folders, rename files and folders, and perform other file management actions.
- Copy, move and delete: You can copy a file or folder to create an identical copy in another location on your computer. You can move a file or folder to move it from one location to another on your computer. You can also delete a file or folder to remove it permanently from your operating system.
- Rename: You can rename a file or folder to change its name. This can be useful for organizing your files in a more meaningful way, or for correcting naming errors.
- File search: Operating systems generally have file search functions that allow you to search for files and folders on your computer according to certain criteria, such as file name, file extension, modification date, etc. This can help you find the files you need quickly and easily. This can help you quickly find the files you need.

It's important to understand the basic concepts of file and folder management in your specific operating system to be able to organize and manage your files and folders effectively on your computer. Each operating system may have specific features and keyboard shortcuts to perform these actions, so it's advisable to consult your operating system's specific documentation to learn more about file and folder management.

CHAPTER 4: INTERNET AND WEB BROWSING

1. Understanding the basics of the Internet

Understanding the basics of the Internet is essential in today's digital world. Here are some basic concepts to help you better understand how the Internet works:

- Internet: The Internet is a worldwide network of interconnected computers using a common communications protocol known as TCP/IP (Transmission Control Protocol/Internet Protocol). It enables information and resources to be shared worldwide, via the World Wide Web (WWW), electronic mail (e-mail), instant messaging, file sharing and much more.

These are just a few basic concepts to help you understand the basics of the Internet.

2. Using a web browser

   Using a web browser is essential for accessing the Internet and browsing websites. Here are the general steps for using a web browser:

- Open browser: Launch the web browser of your choice on your computer, smartphone or tablet. Popular web browsers include Google Chrome, Mozilla Firefox, Microsoft Edge, Safari, and others.

Google Chrome Microsoft Edge Mozila Safaris

- Entering a web address: In the browser's address bar, enter the web address (URL) of the website you wish to visit. Make sure you enter the correct and complete address, including the prefix "http://" or "https://" if necessary.

- Press Enter: Press the "Enter" key on your keyboard or click on the "Go" button in your browser to access the website corresponding to the address entered.

- Navigating the website: Once you've accessed a website, you can navigate its pages using hyperlinks, buttons, menus and other interactive elements of the site. You can also use the browser's navigation buttons to go back, forward, refresh the page, etc.

- Perform interactive actions: On a website, you can perform a variety of interactive actions, such as filling in forms, clicking buttons, sending messages, watching videos, downloading files, and much more. Websites can have different functionalities, depending on their nature and purpose.
- Using browser features: Web browsers also have many built-in features, such as bookmark management, page search, tab management, password management, download management and many more. Familiarize yourself with these features to optimize your browsing experience.
- Respect good security practices: When using a web browser, it's important to respect good online security practices, such as not clicking on suspicious links, not disclosing sensitive information online, using secure connections (https://) whenever possible, and keeping your browser and extensions up to date to protect against security vulnerabilities.

This is a general overview of how to use a web browser. Each browser has its own specific features and functionality, so feel free to explore and familiarize yourself with the one you're using to optimize your web browsing experience.

3. Online search and secure browsing

Online research and secure browsing are important skills for surfing the Internet safely and efficiently. Here are a few key points to bear in mind:

- Use a reliable search engine: Use a reputable and reliable search engine, such as Google or Bing, to carry out your online searches. Avoid clicking on suspicious links or downloading files from untrusted sources.
- Use relevant keywords: When entering search terms into a search engine, use relevant keywords to obtain precise, targeted results. Try to formulate your searches clearly and specifically to obtain the desired results.
- Evaluate sources: When consulting search results, assess the credibility and reliability of sources before taking information at face value. Check the reputation of the website, the expertise of the author, the date of publication, and cross-reference the information with other reliable sources to confirm its accuracy.
- Use secure websites (https): When accessing websites, make sure they use a secure connection (https://) to protect your browsing information. Secure websites encrypt the data exchanged between your browser and the website, offering greater privacy and security.
- Avoid suspicious websites: Avoid visiting suspicious websites, such as those that request sensitive information for no good reason, display inappropriate or questionable content, or appear unreliable. Beware of websites that seem too good to be true, or that ask you for sensitive personal information for no good reason.
- Use an ad blocker: Ads on some websites can be malicious and potentially dangerous to your browsing security. Using an ad blocker can help you minimize the risk of exposure to malicious ads and improve your browsing experience.

- Update your browser and software: Make sure you're always using the latest version of your web browser, as well as keeping your security software, such as antivirus and firewall software, up to date to protect against known security vulnerabilities.
- Avoid disclosing sensitive information: Avoid disclosing sensitive information, such as bank account details, social security numbers, or passwords, online, unless absolutely necessary and you're on a secure, reliable website.

By practicing safe online searching and browsing, you can protect your personal information, avoid suspicious websites and security threats, and enjoy a safer Internet browsing experience. Always be vigilant and use good online security practices to protect your privacy and data.

CHAPTER 5: SOFTWARE AND APPLICATIONS

1. Differences between software and applications

The terms "software" and "application" are often used interchangeably, but can have slightly different meanings depending on the context. Here are some common differences between software and applications:

- Scope and functions: Software is a set of computer programs that can be used to perform a variety of tasks, functions or data processing. It can include several applications grouped together in a single software package. In contrast, an application is a stand-alone computer program designed to perform a specific task or provide a specific functionality, generally intended for use by end-users.
- Platforms and runtime environments: Software can be designed to run on different operating systems (such as Windows, macOS, Linux, etc.) or different types of device (such as desktops, laptops, servers, etc.), while applications are generally designed to run on specific platforms, such as smartphones, tablets, web browsers, etc.
- Complexity and customization: Software can be more complex and offer greater flexibility in terms of customization and configuration, as it is generally designed to meet broader and more varied needs. Applications, on the other hand, are generally designed to be user-friendly and easy to use, with specific features and user interfaces optimized for a particular task or functionality.

- Distribution and installation: Software can be distributed in the form of licenses, packages or software suites, while applications are generally available via application distribution platforms, such as app stores, online stores or developer websites. Applications can be installed and run locally on the user's device, while some software may require more complex installation on a server or network.
- Updates and evolution: Software can be updated periodically to add new features, fix bugs or improve performance, while applications can also benefit from regular updates to maintain their functionality and security. However, applications can also be updated automatically without requiring user intervention, whereas software updates may require manual intervention.

In summary, although the terms "software" and "application" are often used interchangeably, software is generally broader in scope and functionality, can be more complex and customizable, and can be distributed and installed in a variety of ways, whereas applications are generally more specific, designed to run on specific platforms, and are often distributed via application distribution platforms.

2. The main types of software (office, graphics, multimedia, etc.)
   There are several types of software used in specific fields, such as office automation, graphics and multimedia. Here's a list of the main types of software in these fields:

- Office software: This is software used for everyday office tasks, such as creating text documents, spreadsheets, presentations, databases and e-mail programs. Microsoft Office, which includes software such as Word, Excel, PowerPoint and Outlook, is one of the most commonly used examples of office software. Other popular office suites include Google Workspace (formerly G Suite), LibreOffice and Apple iWork.

- Graphics software: This is software used for creating and manipulating images and graphics, such as photos, illustrations, designs, animations and videos. Adobe Creative Cloud is one of the most widely used graphic design software suites, including popular applications such as Photoshop, Illustrator, InDesign, Premiere Pro and After Effects. Other popular graphics software includes GIMP, CorelDRAW, Sketch and Canva.

- Multimedia software: Software used to create, manage and manipulate multimedia content, such as images, videos, sounds and animations. Software for video editing, audio editing, photo retouching and animation creation are included in this category. Examples of commonly used multimedia software include Adobe Premiere Pro, Final Cut Pro, Audacity, VLC Media Player, and Blender.

It's important to note that there are many other types of specialized software in other fields, such as development software, project management software, computer-aided design (CAD) software, content management software (CMS), security software, network software, educational software, and many more. The diversity of software available reflects the wide variety of needs and applications in the IT field.

3. Software installation and use

Software installation and use may vary depending on the operating system you're using and the type of software you wish to install. Here are the general steps for installing and using software:

- Downloading the software: You must first download the software from a reliable source, such as the developer's official website or a secure application store.
- Software installation: Once the software has been downloaded, you need to install it on your computer. Double-click on the downloaded installation file and follow the on-screen instructions to install the software. You may be asked to accept the software's terms and conditions, choose an installation location and configure other settings.
- Software configuration: After installation, you may be asked to configure the software by providing additional information, such as creating a user account, setting preferences, or activating licenses.
- Using the software: Once the software is installed and configured, you can use it by following the software's specific instructions. This may include creating new documents, importing or modifying existing files, using the software's features, and many other actions depending on the type of software you're using.

It is important to note that some software may require administrative authorizations to be installed or used, particularly on certain operating systems such as Windows. Make sure you have the necessary authorizations and follow the instructions for installing and using the software to avoid any problems.

It's also advisable to always download software from reliable sources to avoid the risk of malware or viruses. Read user reviews, check the reputation of the software developer and make sure you download the latest versions of the software to benefit from security updates and new features.

CHAPTER 6: COMPUTER SECURITY

1. Understanding computer threats (viruses, malware, phishing, etc.)

IT threats are actions or events that can compromise the security, integrity, confidentiality or availability of data and IT systems.

There are many forms of computer threats, including :

- Viruses, worms and malware: These are computer programs designed to cause damage to a computer, network or data. They can spread from one system to another, infecting files and causing malfunctions or data loss.

Computer virus to computer malware

- Denial of service attacks (DDoS): These are attacks designed to render a service or website unavailable by flooding the target system with excessive traffic, causing the system to overload and go offline.

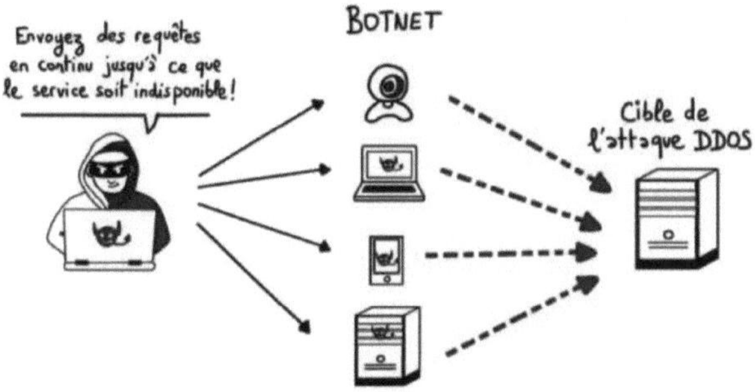

- Hacking: Unauthorized access to a computer system or network with the aim of stealing, altering or destroying data, or obtaining an illegal advantage.

- Phishing: This is an attack technique used to obtain sensitive information, such as login credentials, passwords or financial information, by posing as a trusted entity.

- Computer espionage: The monitoring or interception of an individual's, company's or organization's electronic communications without their consent, usually in order to obtain confidential information.

- Malware and: These are programs designed to collect information about a user's activities, monitor their online actions, or obtain sensitive information without their consent.

- Social engineering: This involves manipulating or deceiving individuals to obtain confidential information or gain access to computer systems by exploiting users' trust or negligence.

It's important to understand these computer threats and take steps to protect your systems and data. This can include using anti-virus software and firewalls, regularly updating your software and operating systems with the latest security patches, educating users about computer security and implementing best security practices, such as using strong passwords, regularly backing up data and checking sources before downloading files or clicking on links.

2. Tips for protecting your computer and data

Protecting your computer and data is essential to ensuring the security of your personal and professional information. Here are some tips on how to protect your computer and data:

- Use antivirus software: Install reliable antivirus software and make sure you keep it regularly updated. It will help you detect and remove viruses, malware and other potential threats.

- Use a firewall: A firewall is a security barrier that protects your computer from unauthorized access from the Internet. Make sure you have a firewall enabled on your computer to block unwanted access attempts.

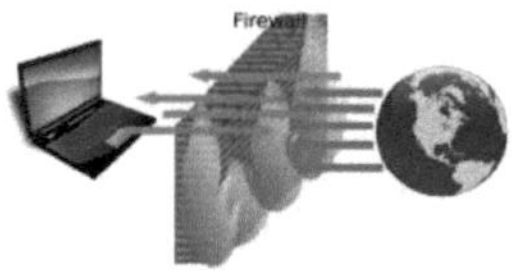

- Software: Make sure your software, including your operating system, web browsers, applications and plug-ins, are regularly updated with the latest security patches. Updates often contain important security patches to close known vulnerabilities.

- Use strong passwords: Use complex, unique passwords for your online accounts, including access to your computer. Avoid using passwords that are easy to guess, such as names of family members or dates of birth, and don't use the same password for multiple accounts.

Beware of suspicious e-mails and links: Don't click on links or open emails from unknown or suspicious senders. Beware of email requests for personal or financial information, as these could be phishing attempts.

- Back up your data regularly: Make regular backups of your important data on external media or in a secure online storage service. This will enable you to recover your data in the event of loss, malware attack or hardware failure.

Secure online storage.

- Be vigilant online: Be aware of what you share online and avoid divulging sensitive personal information, such as your social security number, bank details or identification details, unless you are sure of the legitimacy of the website or the person with whom you are sharing this information.

- Use additional security tools: In addition to anti-virus and firewall software, you can also use other additional security tools, such as anti-malware software, ad blockers, privacy tools, etc., to strengthen your computer's security.

By following these tips and adopting good computer security practices, you can help protect your computer and your data from computer threats. It's also important to keep abreast of the latest trends in computer security, and to update your knowledge regularly to better protect yourself online.

3. Managing passwords and sensitive data

Managing passwords and sensitive data is an essential part of IT security. Here are a few tips to help you manage your passwords and sensitive data securely:

- Use strong passwords: Use complex, unique passwords for every online account you have. Avoid using passwords that are easy to guess, such as words from the dictionary, names of family members or personal information. Instead, opt for long passwords, with a combination of letters, numbers, symbols and special characters.
- Don't share your passwords: Never share your passwords with others unless absolutely necessary and secure. Don't write them down on post-it notes or send them by email or text message. Instead, use secure password management solutions to store and manage your passwords securely.
- Enable two-factor authentication: Two-factor authentication (2FA) adds an extra layer of security to your accounts by requiring a second form of identification, in addition to your

password, usually in the form of a unique code sent to your phone or generated by an application. Always activate two-factor authentication whenever possible to reinforce the security of your accounts.

- Avoid storing sensitive data on your computer or in the cloud: Avoid storing sensitive data, such as financial information, social security numbers, copies of passports or other sensitive data on your computer or in the cloud, unless really necessary. If you must store such data, be sure to encrypt it and store it in secure, password-protected locations.
- Beware of suspicious e-mails and websites: Beware of e-mails or websites that ask you for sensitive information, even if they appear genuine. Always check the authenticity of the sender and the website before providing sensitive information. Avoid clicking on suspicious links in e-mails or on social networks.
- Make regular back-ups of your sensitive data: Make regular back-ups of your sensitive data on external media or in a secure online storage service. This will enable you to recover your data in the event of loss, theft or hardware failure.
- Use encryption: Use encryption to protect your sensitive data when it's stored or transferred. Encryption ensures that your data is encoded and cannot be read without the appropriate decryption key.

By following these best practices, you can better protect your passwords and sensitive data against potential threats, and strengthen the security of your personal and business information online.

MIX
Papier aus verantwortungsvollen Quellen
Paper from responsible sources
FSC® C105338

Printed by Books on Demand GmbH, Norderstedt / Germany